T0087931

GEIS

CAITRÍONA O'REILLY

Geis

WAKE FOREST UNIVERSITY PRESS

WAKE FOREST UNIVERSITY PRESS

Post Office Box 7333

Winston-Salem, NC 27109

wfupress.wfu.edu

ISBN 978-1-930630-73-4

Library of Congress Catalog Number 2014956948

First published in 2015 by Bloodaxe Books Ltd., UK

Designed and typeset by Quemadura

Cover illustration: Madeline von Foerster, *Invasive Species II*, 2008.

Used with permission of the artist.

FOR SIMON DURRANT

CONTENTS

Ovum

1

Island

2

Spanish Fly

5

Amanita Virosa

7

Ariadne

8

Empty House

10

Comparative Mythography

12

Geis

14

The Winter Suicides

23

Snow

24

Polar

26

Iceland

28

The Gardener

29

The Servant Question

31

The Antikythera Mechanism

35

Baltic Amber

37

Blue Poles

39

Clotho

41

Autotomy

42

*The Man with No Name
as Vital Principle: A Ghazal*

44

Chiune Sugihara

46

The Airship Era

47

An Idea of Iowa

49

Everything Flowers

50

Bee on Agastache

52

Triptych

54

August on Dungeness

60

Potlatch

62

Komorebi

63

NOTES

65

ACKNOWLEDGEMENTS

67

GEIS

Ovum

You'd take it for zero, or nothing,
or the spotless oval your lips make saying it,
as if you blew both yolk and albumen
through its pin-pricked head: the meat
of the word made orotund and Latinate.
It's like putting your mouth to the smooth
breast of the ocarina, from *oca*, the goose,
hooting out its fledgling notes.
Unless you seal the gap it's left, they'll fall
out, those other o-words, like bubbles
streaming through a soapy blow-hole:
from *oblation* and *obloquy* to *oxlip* and *ozone*,
and that sneaky Trojan *obol*,
coin-shaped, it's true, but spawned
from the spiky Greek of *obelus*,
the death-mark, dagger or crucifix,
as phallic and obvious, now that you say it,
as that double o in spermatozoon,
which enters by its own locomotion—
the flagellum, its tiny whip and scourge.

Island

I. MIRROR

I recognised her in your eyes,
that way you have of keeping separate,
aware that to wake is to weigh the damage.
From the shore of my own island I saw
her in the shards of your face,
as though she'd shattered her mirror
and left the pieces there to glitter.
Brightness attracts me like a child:
the light-veined sea,
and the threads of light from the sky,
and you whom I see but cannot reach,
intangible as phosphor blooming on water,
cold as the dawn of our one waking.

2. HUNGER

Beyond the throw of any rope,
head full of the skua's laughter,
I faced the reeling shore.
You've left me thin with saintly hunger,
fed me renunciation's delicate bread.
My chief want:
the gold-and-olive chasing of your glance,
a look of nakedness and clear fathoms.
The crystal spider hidden in your eye
cast a single lucent cord,
hung between us the quivering instant,
then shrank to spinning veils.
It pierced me the way light pierces
the tunnel in a tunnel-grave:
only to distinguish the dark.

3. VIATICUM

Forgetfulness
goes on with our clothes,
all the discreet lies.

We'll discard the details:
your tongue scouring my mouth,
our voices, our hands, our selves.

Still it hums along my veins—
a view I took from the hill
that to you was usual—

beaches gleaming with northern birds,
the wing-bones and skulls
of the waves' whitest outcasts.

It is bread for the hungry road.
The island is a flower head,
and the swaying sea its stem.

Spanish Fly

Not glass-green at all but iridescent,
a mineral-winged insect pulverised

with toads' bones, moles' teeth and iron filings;
a glittering suspension I give him to drink,

unknowing, for what he's made me see:
not the globe but the map's foxed edges,

not the sentence but the syllable,
not the embroidery but the unpicked stitch.

Yesterday the moon was a beehive
among the swarming constellations;

I thought, *the universe is full of gods.*
Today it is smashed atoms and dust.

Overhead, the voice of the aeroplane drops
an interval, and I know fear.

From him I learned my life is chemical,
sub rosa; that that is how it is lived.

I twist silently in my cell.
For every antidote there is a poison:

mad honey of rhododendron
dripping its amber beads, cantharidin or ergot.

Hourly now I wait for news;
the clock's tick is an itch.

Amanita Virosa

Filament on filament
below your feet, its fine-meshed web's
mycelium, its net.
Above all: know your enemy.
A nub pushing the crumbled loam
aside, a fruiting
blue-white, white-gilled body: erotic,

spilling its fine white powders;
its pale spore-print the negative
of a moth's dense-celled wing.
Cauled in a universal veil
and crowning past the tight membrane:
the soft cranium,
the ragged annulus emerging.

To be brushed by the least wing-
tip, the feathered edge of a gill,
ignites in the cell's
integument the sacred fire.
It is her silent spreading gift,
tiny destroyer:
her colourlessness, her bone-white chrism.

Ariadne

What seemed
a simple structure
is not so now.

O house—
device to conceal
the obscene:

end-stopped corridors
sprout like horns
and shut me in;

walls of hide
stifle my cries
loud as Pasiphae's

whose bull-headed baby
tore her breast.
There's a smell

of sex and sulphur—
the atmosphere
of rutting's recent.

Some beast
left ample evidence
on the sheets—

stains
hymenal or menstrual,
underwear scattered

across the floor.
It will take me a lifetime
to unpick this,

finding the right thread
to pull and unravel,
pull and unravel.

Empty House

I am a blank harvest.
The cat's cry haunts me—
what does it remind me of?

Each word inscribed
masks the silence
of a seed-bed gone to seed.

A house can stand
too long neglected:
details we've shed,

grey rains of scurf,
gather like thistledown
under the bed

where occur
such sterile irrigations.
A skin of rubber

saves us from each other.
Nothing gets through,
but at night the traitor body

dreams itself full
of death-in-life
and life-in-death:

stillborn,
furled beneath my ribs.
Morning delivers me

silently.
Rain leaks from between
my folded lids.

Comparative Mythography

Each day brings less to believe.
Once, men with ichor in their veins,
knowing their souls were made

of polished atoms
and greatly fearing emptiness,
filled the spaces on their vases

with swastika and lotus.
A hare inhabited the moon:
three seas made its head and ears,

its tail was a sea of clouds.
Where serpents squirmed inside
the world's slit belly,

Metztli, lowliest god of worms,
failed to become the sun
and became instead the moon,

his pallor shadowed by a hare.
Coatlicue was his violent sister,
digging the graves of her children

with ragged fingernails,
wearing for her necklace
their hearts and hands and skulls.

The shrieking god of night and owls
was Chalchiuhtecolotl;
of obloquy and cold stone,

Itztlacoliuhqui-Ixquimilli,
who filled the known universe
with his seething body,

his seething name.
Each day brings less, now,
to believe. Knowledge means

not that it is true, but that it works:
the elimination of air in a jar
makes smoke trickle downwards,

boils cool water,
silences the tongues of bells.
It takes the strength of sixteen horses

to part a pair of bronze hemispheres
with nothing between them,
thus proving that nothing exists.

Geis

I. OUR LADY OF THE DRY TREE

It was a sickness, this love I imagined
descending in a feathered storm,
in a drench of illumined leaves.

And I was a bird, hedge-snared
on a trunk of writhing stone,
nervous with looking through desire's dry cage,

a skeleton grid of branches hung
with signs of my devising.
Love was never here. That is the truth

for one who feeds on shadows,
on the wafer's feverish penumbra,
on her own breast's blue milk.

II. NIGHT SWEAT

Once the descent begins it is hard to stop.
Like a night-flying pilot in his little plane,
my instruments give warnings,
but the dreams that swallow me are medieval:

pointed flames out of Bosch
scorch me hotter
than any bitch burned by history.
It is one drenched waking after another.

Now I am straddled by a great night bird,
a muscular talon to each hip bone.
How I struggle to bear him up:
his soaked wings hover.

III. LEAVEN

An old lady wanders the ward,
a lost comet.
Nothing reaches her in her orbit.

Her knuckles are hung with rings.
Her nostrils are crimson-ringed.
White waxen brows; wrists of wax.

Nosing the bones of her distraction,
she wanders.
Purple jumps beneath her skin:

throat of an amphibian.
Soon, through her wrinkled mouth,
the ghost of a bird will depart.

She'll barely notice this.
The wind will send its green flame
flickering over the grass.

IV. GEIS

I bruise my knuckles
against its smooth white walls.

Containment is in
the nature of a house,

but I would sooner
the berserker's filthy pelt,

sooner swallow hot coals
as proof against the blunt

force of iron, sooner a door
in the two-chambered brain

to let the dark in still
and through which the owl

might issue its summons.
The wound of the mouth closes.

To perish its roots
a radiant stone is placed on the tongue.

V. O

is getting the cramped brain
to release its grip,

is prising open its fingers.
Stiff petals, wet wrinkled wings

coil around nothing,
like the foetus its long past.

Morning bruises the horizon;
pain departs like a ship.

And the drug is almost love
as the day is almost blue:

veins glisten with slippery balm.
Then I am spilled scatheless

from the casing dark:
as the river splits itself on a stone;

as the tree swallows a stone
and in greenness continues.

VI. ISOLATE BUT PRESERVE

The order almost came too late,
already the pulse was idling.
I'd listened too long
to the boy on the closed ward
charge the doors with his head,
the girl whose thoughts
had caused her cousin's cancer.
There were dead baby dreams.
There was no one.

A January afternoon up on the Spink
the year contracted to a glacial point
between two hills.
Low on the mauve horizon
a single star ignited icily.
I felt the greenness rise in my throat.

Isolate but preserve:
the head of a dissected body still might sing,
its mouth still utter bright notes,
almost the way a captive might
writhe free of his captors,
leaving them astonished,
grasping his empty coat.

VII. RIDDLE

It is a purple knot of violence in the head;
that old snarl in the brain again that will not unfurl.
It is the white-gloved master of lies and what he said.
It is two months in a sweat-soaked hospital bed.
It is the curse swallowed before it is told.
It is the mirror at which a hundred glass hammers are hurled.
It is the seed in its socket at the year's death.
It is two grass blades and a stone.
It is one use to which a warm bath can be put.
It is to discern in scattered light the dark,
its particulates adhering to the world like soot.
It is all the stuttering truths the throat can hold.
It is the sapling coating itself in rings.
It is the splinter the mantle blunts with pearl.

VIII. JONAH

The silver-limbed birch at my window:
its leaves glitter and spin.
Under the wind they heave like the sea.
What is rumoured by the movement of these branches?
The way a word unlatches a door,
the way the cathedral on the hill puts me in mind of a high ship?
To refuse is not to live.

> *The waters compassed me about, even to the soul: the depth*
> *closed me round about, the weeds were wrapped about my head.*

The clattering backwash and undertow of a life!
A darkness swallowed me whole.
I subsisted in its guts, in a foetal coil,
my skin blanched by its acids,
my limbs attenuated as a seedling kept from the light.
It was no gothic, ringing interior, this;
I was held close, familiar.
Its tissues muffled my cries.

Brothers, we who have gone down to the roots of the mountain,
and have seen the worm bite the gourd's root,
are sea-changed, and see with the light behind us,

as through a fine membrane,
a thin curtain of isinglass,
the floaters drifting in our eyes like ghosts.
Brothers, to refuse is not to live.
The world has eaten us the way the world must.

The Winter Suicides

They ask and the world gives them a stone,
inclining her head towards the darkness.

Out among the night stations the signals falter,
the mechanism of the cell winds down.

We can do nothing now but watch, wait and watch,
leaving them to the winds, the drag of tides,

who lately were apt to brood upon themselves and hatch
a rope, a hook, a chair, a bell, a solicitude;

rarely a kindness. To themselves they were least kind.
Like us, they were unable to believe

the frequencies of light concerned them;
they followed the logic of the particle down

to the sea floor, literalists who sought a solution.
In the silence, in the immeasurable interval

between systole and dawn, we ask:
she gives us the snowdrop's sidereal pallor.

Snow

What is it to talk about silence?
When I look up from my table

it will still be there
where it fell in the night,

hurrying to congregate
in the cone cast by the street lamp,

and in the darkness, the others,
unseen but legion.

How bruise-blue the shadows
on the garden

and the frozen cobwebs
snapped beneath their weight.

In the park we blundered
across it, the quiet,

in spite of its exclamatory outline
on bare trees,

down great hushed halls of white
and the white lake picked out in kanji

by the moorhen's feet.
Are there words for what I felt

in the faceted garden?
Motes, corpuscles, animalcules.

And it is a relief to feel it touch me
with its meaning,

its vast multitudinous silence,
again and again.

Polar

THE US GEOLOGICAL SURVEY PREDICTS
TWO-THIRDS OF THE WORLD'S POLAR BEARS
WILL DISAPPEAR BY 2050

By means of this the photon
is deflected into darkness,
our white-heat leaking from us.

A great absconded god of emptiness
hunted the groaning floes,
scattering waves and particles from his coat,

his hair hollow as birds' bones.
Intervals of immense, glittering distance.
Then the animal-heat of fur,

of blood and membrane, and hot breath,
the black-tongued breath of the sea.
He tasted the breath of whales,

he haunted the boundaries—
ice-rim and earth-rim; the whetstone sky
on which scents sharpened,

on which his breath hung its own strange statues.
Mage of the edge,
who knew his material in all its aspects,

this yearly raising of dense liquid
to frazil, nilas and pack-ice;
its boundless transformations.

Always, he was equal to the whiteness
of his kingdom; totem and numen
to a universe now present, now absent.

Who will bury him like the Chukchi,
his huge head indicating true north,
amid libations and the pouring out of oil?

Iceland

FOR SIMON

Not that the landscape was hourly altered by small quakes,
or that rainbows were suspended about the scalding air,
        or that the dropped coin turned
        and glittered too long in the fissure;

but that I lost my footing on the path to the frozen water-
fall, and you were not yet there. Even my breath was taken
        on that deafening morning,
        in an absence of trees.

The Gardener

The menu warned that fish caught locally
may contain dangerous levels of cadmium
and isotopes—or was it allotropes?—
I didn't care . . .

That night, after the lecture,
I sweated through dinner with a clever man
who displayed his cleverness decorously,
like the secretary bird its quills.
Did he notice the beads glistening in my philtrum
like the shine off the poisoned Pacific?

And I wondered what dangerous dust I had inhaled,
to make my breath so difficult,
as I lay in the cheap hotel on Kearny Street,
counting the notches on a plastic thermometer
and feverishly dialling your number
across half the blacked-out globe.

Earlier, I'd looked for pelicans on Alcatraz Island
and seen none, and tried to imagine
the suffering of the celebrity hoodlum
contemplating the saved in their bliss
across the deadly strait, in the eternal city.

The phone rang out twice in the empty house
as it had rung out so often in that other house,
and my panic was almost theatrical
until your voice, warm and close,
reminded me again of the notes I'd made
of the words of the island's only gardener:

I kept no record of my failures,
and there were many. . . . The main thing
was to assure some success by trying many things
and holding onto those plants which had learned
that life is worth holding onto,
even at its bitterest.

The Servant Question

A most unlikely housemaid
or maid-of-all-work you must have been,
you with your carefree attitude
to kitchen hygiene,
intensified on a whim
but witnessed mainly by the thickening slick
of grease on your press tops
and tea leaf-choked plughole.

Your spidery script survives
on my kitchen jars to this day:
Jam, Tea, Sugar, Flour (Self-Raising).

I have been laughing along with Woolf
at her refractory chars:
Lottie was it,
or Nellie (never a surname);
always carping on about their insides,
resentful and swart-eyed,
superstitious as children.

I read:
It strikes me that one is absurd to expect

good temper or magnanimity from servants,
considering what crowded small rooms they live in,
with their work all about them.

I imagine you at sixteen
dispatched to Belfast to do for the quality;
auburn, green-eyed,
a little dreamy and clumsy.

Mornings, when you had finished
with the dusting and flowers,
you soothed your homesickness
by picking out one-fingered airs on the piano,
resting your forehead against its lid,
inhaling the beeswax and roses.

Caught dawdling and upbraided,
that's how it went,
the hearth needed blacking,
the fender polishing.

You blushed at seventy to recall
the priceless string of Mikimoto pearls
discovered beneath the stockings and rosary
in your top drawer,
you who stole nothing your whole life,

but the mistress wanted you gone
and one can blame a servant for anything:
smeared decanters, chipped china, cracked plate,
even the sidelong attentions
of the household's eldest son.

Your mother took your dismissal
with resignation and a sign of the cross;
by then the long shadow
of the workhouse had dwindled,
and a pretty girl could do well
provided she was careful.

She had—husbandless but resourceful—
collected rainwater
to improve your complexion
following those nights spent
scrubbing the parochial hall floor
for a few shillings after dances.

The Protestant doctor,
pleased with her cooking,
enjoined her for weeks
to give her children to the orphanage
and live in. Her calm reply:
she would take her babies to the river first
and drown them.

Relenting, he considered that after all
the woman must care for her children,
who were good little things
admittedly, polite,
well-dressed and well-fed.

That child you were is long dead,
in a drowned epoch
of old maids and bookish, disappointed women.
Bluish and rain-glazed, these objects
cast up like the river's bleached tenants
into a level landscape
are not my memories,
yet they move in me continually
with a river's moment,
breaking and reforming its ripples, its patterns,
through all my rooms and days,
my work all about me.

The Antikythera Mechanism

Too subtle to have been unique, a circular system
of fine-toothed gears in cedar, its wheeled delicate
copper-alloy movement, cranked by a handle, clicks and whirrs

so its incised texts rotate. This year: *the colour is black,* or
the colour is fire-red. Almost overlooked, dredged
through starless ages by a sponge-diver crippled by the bends,

the sea-bitten glyphs, friable as icing, say that knowledge is dust
almost, but this is the moon in a groove;
no vagabond, but modest and observable in all her pale steps

and lunations. Watching her narrow smile snagged
on the needle tip of the cypress, or floating brokenly
on a sea which admitted darkness but was never blue

must have suggested to him this gleaming planetary gearing,
since to cast bronze is to pray, and to beat metal is to give praise.
There was time in the town-square clepsydra but it trickled away,

he could never step into it again. These were the loved hours:
the poem of the moment, of pouring ripeness, when the breeze
drove the flame of its exact pattern across the corn.

Wallingford's world-famous astrolabe, Su Song's Cosmic Engine,
all the beauty of escapements—mercury, grasshopper or deadlock—
even the ticking decay in nine billion caesium cycles

interrogate, like this drowned analect of a mechanical age,
ever more precisely the same silence. *Shall I find it?*
Shall I become rich? Shall I live an object of envy?

Shall I die in my bed? But nothing, since the nice-fingered craftsmen
of Corinth set the gear-trains to a careful stargazer's design,
has come close to an answer. Consult the oracle bones,

cast the yarrow stalks, inhale the fine particles of your trade
until they glitter in lung and bone. It is the distant ignition of stars:
you, this clock, this dust. The *yes-no, no-yes* of the pendulum.

Baltic Amber

Rational Pliny considered it
an emetic property of the sea

beached with the whale's
disgorged ambergris

after an ice-choked winter.
But for the Greeks it meant the sun.

A falling star, a shattered axle-tree;
Phaëthon, that original boy-racer,

crashed and burned.
His sisters, in the immense

geological time of their grief,
turned into ginkgos, living fossils

exuding buttery tears,
swallowing blossoms,

small frogs, feathers, insects
with pollen grains on their wings.

Rubbing it imparts a charge
that anchors all light-bodied things

to its particled heart,
as if it secreted the light's properties

in its bubbling interior:
elektron, bony amber,

Eocene sun
between finger and thumb.

Blue Poles

AFTER JACKSON POLLOCK

Freedom is a prison for the representative savant
    addled on bath-tub gin and with retinas inflamed
from too long staring into the Arizona sun
    or into red dirt which acknowledges no master
but the attrition of desert winds and melt-water.
    Is that why you cast such desperate lariats
across space, repeatedly anticipating the fall
    into disillusion, the sine wave skewered
by the oscilloscope, the mirror's hairline fracture?
    The West was won and there was nowhere left to go
so you vanished into a dream of perpetual motion
    knowing that once to touch the surface
was to break the spell, but that while the colours hung
    on the air an instant, there was no such thing
as the pushy midwife, the veiled mother in the photograph,
    the rich woman's bleated blandishments.
Tracing the drunken white line at midnight on the highway,
    you were too far gone to contemplate return,
like Crowhurst aboard the *Electron;* not meaning
    to go to sea, but drawing about you

such a field of force that there was nothing left to do
    but plant blue poles among the spindrift and iron filings
and step, clutching your brass chronometer,
    clean off the deck and into the sky
where a lens rose to meet you like a terrifying eye.

Clotho

AFTER CAMILLE CLAUDEL

And in the end it was easiest to let go
of all that vigilance, the endless distaff-to-spindle rigour
of your compulsions, and allow the silks to snarl.
For a while, perhaps, you struggled to escape,

snared like an insect in your own allurements.
You had never believed that life was what happened to us.
Rather it was to strike sparks from stone repeatedly,
smoothing the planes with a morsel of bone

until your own eyes glittered in the veined torso.
For here there is no place that does not see you . . .
You were a wilful girl, and wilful girls must learn
that to haul life from matter is a god's concern.

And always there was something there you could not reach:
it flickered below the surface of the marble
like a candle behind a grimed window,
mocking your eager questions like an echo.

Autotomy

For years I have sought to know
what the quiver tree

wordlessly comprehends.
On the Namib plain

the thickened air emits a shriek
fine as bats' ultrasound

that is the frequency of heat,
of the burning life

with which it has come to terms.
I should like one day to see it

tight-skinned, thickly powdered
as de Pompadour.

Cumbersome, oedemic,
it bears its heavy inflorescence

like a witness to some
continual atrocity;

or else, in the way of tongue-cut women
(Lavinia, Philomel)

it amputates what is most precious,
then quickly seals the wound

so that the scar no longer shows;
the stumps smooth as sea-washed bone.

The Man with No Name

as Vital Principle: A Ghazal

Eastwood as No-Name in *A Fistful of Dollars*.
The town called Apricots is built of whitewashed adobe.

Behind the walls are widows, staring their tragic arias. Nothing here flowers
   or fruits.
There is the ringer of the dead-bell, the sprightly coffin-maker.

Something looks through the Stranger's eyes, looking. It is a secret.
It is life in this town of death. The Stranger does not speak it.

Things solidify from their names. Where the empty sky was, there is smoke,
and from this comes the figure of the Stranger whose name is smoke.

Eastwood *contrapposto*. He understands the exact gesture
is a pattern of immortality, and that evil has an element of smirk.

He is a hat, a cheroot, a serape with strange signs.
He is the *Son of Man*, bowler-hatted, an apple where his face should be.

After the beating, after his high-hipped, sidewinder crawl through the dirt,
he is not ashamed to go in the guise of death. Pride is a part of what he has
   left behind.

On the third day he emerges from the mineshaft. The stone rolled back . . .
His body folds, like a spider's, under each attack.

Still he comes. Under the drunken parabola of the sun he watches himself
    turn,
reflected in the eye of his enemy, from a speck of dust into a man.

Chiune Sugihara

The customs had altered again.
Men to whom violence gave a face
had decided that this time force

would have a quantifiable outcome,
their iron-link logic exact as clocks.
You understood their language.

The lines of dusty desperate people
lengthened outside your gate
like shadows in August.

Impossible to parse a motive
in the abecedary of your act,
to know whether your eyes were kind

as you waited in overcoat and trilby
at the station in Kaunas. Some just know
that love must be put into action or it is not love:

a chain of delicate characters under
your swift, unhesitant brush;
so many parched buds unfurling in ink.

The Airship Era

They'd barely emerged from the deep green forests
of that epauletted century. Geraniums bloomed on windowsills in
   Heidelberg.
Student princes eyed the tavernkeeper's daughter through the blond foam
of their tankards. The future must have seemed weightless
as it came nosing through the clouds, smooth as a biblical fish
throwing its giant shadow on the sea floor, its thin gold-beater's skin
pressed back against its ribs, cloche-hatted women in fox furs
waving through its observation windows. Composed of too much

dream-stuff to be *echt matériel*, shoals of them congregated silently
over London in the moon's dark phases, concealed above clouds.
Their crews were unnerved by crackling blue haloes; eerie lightning
shot from frostbitten fingers as they lowered spy baskets
on trapeze wires below the cloud cover, taking careful soundings,
then dropped their antique payloads on the gaping population.
Those whom they did not kill scarcely believed in them,
improbable contraptions the parchment-yellow colour of old maps,

vessels a rational traveller might have chosen, a half-century earlier,
to pursue daft, round-the-world steampunk wagers. But for them—
the gilded aerialists in their giant dirigibles—the world remained a
   storybook

unfolding endlessly in signs and wonders, over which they drifted
in stylish accidie; leviathan-hunters, relaxed as Victorian naturalists.
And up there everything looked different:
the borders absurd, the people in their witch-fearing villages as out-of-date
as peasants in a medieval breviary. The mountains, too, seemed
    surpassable,

offering an alternative angle on the sublime. Occasionally there was
    concern:
a tear in the fabric, hooked to a typhoon's tail above the China Sea,
or harried by storms across the Atlantic. But how lighter than air they
    were.
They did not understand, as they fell continually upwards,
how the nature of the element was the price of their rising:
the assiduous atom seeking an exit, thronging the fabric of their cells.
Witness was the privilege of the many: newsreels captured the death of
    a star
and—*oh the humanity!*—its last leisurely plummet in fire, its ashen
    armature.

An Idea of Iowa

Who in their bleakest hour has not considered Iowa?
We live in a place where everything leans in

as if to confide in us, and learn, too late, it is a trick:
the frieze, the whole entablature must topple,

as the drunk on the bus, in the course of his life story,
anoints us with cidery spittle, as the ash

from a thousand fag-end sunsets settles on us.
But Iowa. A darkening indigo shimmer above tracts of corn,

yellow as far as the eye can see, yellow as the sun
in a child's first drawing, as the cere of the bald eagle

hanging with locked wings on thermals.
Iowa is rising. Free of the deadweight of ice,

it gains an inch a year, a vast loaf proving.
Who first thought of it? (Indian grass, prairie moonwort,

the Pleistocene snail? A place where wars are fought for honey?)
Named for a people asleep, a people with dusty faces,

even its hills are so much dust: loess, the millennial
accumulation of cracked flood-plains; winds.

Everything Flowers

I was reminded of that time we watched the wolf spider
retrieve its pod of thickened silk, appalled more by the hint

of mind in it than by a sense of its primitive hydraulics,
its twin ganglia, book lungs and valved spigots.

What was it you quoth? *Two possibilities exist:*
either we are alone in the universe or we are not.

Both are equally terrifying.
How apposite, I thought. How *grand guignol*.

This morning it just seemed practical.
After an injurious Spring—what can have had such a cold beginning?—

I note the vermilion nipples of the pelargonium,
and our predecessors' aquilegia, that is both eagle and dove

(hiding its imperial lights inside a cottage border);
the bank of bird's foot trefoil that could be writ large

in some twee floriography, were I so inclined,
but mostly how the weakest of them emerge

like stars out of the killing distance
and the vacuum that is their inheritance

unsentimentally, each according to its ability,
though it had seemed unlikely.

Bee on Agastache

It is our calling to be lost in detail:
the peduncle with its cunning bracts, ramified

for the parsing of winged grammarians;
we thrive in the trickery of constructions,

in the manner of address, entry,
the faint trace of civet that was left:

the flower
matches our obsessions exactly.

We have little time for aesthetics:
our schema will not permit it. The viscous air

sustains our humming thoraces on charged paths,
our pile fascinates the very dust, we probe endlessly,

we comb the dust into our grooved tibia.
The groove is. We hold no memory

of our ungrooved selves, those exuviae.
Our rich hours pass on high towers of infloration,

checking the spiralled bracts for petals.
Our calling demands we verify, verify, verify.

When the air cools and thins we cling on,
our stalled limbs' torpor is of the darkness also;

it brushes us with its tumbling dust
and dries to white like salt.

Triptych

AT LINCOLN CATHEDRAL

I. WEST FRONT

There was infinity to build
and soft blond stone in abundance
to be hauled out of the sides of the hill.

The frieze was an alphabet to the unlettered.
Through its broken typeface you can just make out
those leering demons at the corners of your life

leaning into space above the blind arcades.
Time has bleached them
like the blank statues of Greece:

there's Dives in hell, and Lazarus
laughing his carefully calibrated last laugh.
Nine centuries of rain

have dissolved the grooved promises
but left us the demons still.
Is this the unquenchable instinct, to be compelled to ask,

where the answer would deny
both question and questioner?
The world enfolds its being and will not yield,

like an oyster closing on pearl,
or those calm figures in Van der Weyden
reposing in the evening of pure certainty

with folded hands,
upon whose mild, inward-looking faces rests,
very gently, the strange-angled light.

II. NAVE

The woods have lapsed into leaf
almost imperceptibly: unfolding,

just below the rim of vision,
their unseen, light-gathering hands,

as though the trees had dreamed them
and upheld the dream for a time.

This pillared hush lets go
the held breath of winter

and from here to the great nave
of the upturned bark, or boat,

is a transliteration, a declension merely.
The stone trunks that soar to the clerestory

and fan across the roof
still wait on presence.

Is it the backless depth of forests,
the tangled brake

from which the hind crashed, that morning
when I saw the black flash of her eye

and did not understand what I was seeing?
Is there a god of the gaps, and is it

of the interstices between trees
only, and of what might breathe there?

III. BELL TOWER

All lines converge in the eye of the falcon.
Her harsh cries wreathe the bell tower
from her scrape on the high sill.

At cost I have attained my own small vertical,
but the peregrine views all life thus:
at its heart a precipice, a continual launching.

She measures her prey from a serene angle,
the way a stargazer averts his gaze
to see the dimmer stars.

Morning threads its light through her eye's fovea;
she spirals clockwise, cloaked in the sun,
knowing a curved path more true than a straight one.

To see is to grasp; to see is to taste—
killing an empty ceremony sealed in blood
for an act already done.

Like the tail of a meteorite,
I find only a blaze of breast feathers across the ride,
a wind-exposed ribcage.

All lines converge in the eye of the falcon,
in the shape on the bell tower, in the sickle-shadow
that hangs unmoving on the air, yet closes in.

August on Dungeness

Everything inclines upwards
this solar month—
by the sea-wall
even the sunflower's face

is exhausted, observing all summer
plumes of pale gas
ignite in the upper air;
the blood behind our eyelids

like murex-dipped cloth
darkens against the glare;
in days named for conquest
the printed shadows of leaves

shiver and burn
and the sea-kale and sea-poppy
vulcanise among the shingle
on the hot shore;

inside its silent shell, the reactor
follows a chain of consequence
down to the end,
to the very end of the land,

a burnout; a culmination:
it is a desert station
it leaves the taste of its salt wind
on our lips and on our skin.

Potlatch

Since what we have become folds over us
in days and years as involute as petals,

keeping us separate as we pass
on the stairs, or in the kitchen, or in close conversation,

so it becomes necessary and formal,
this other language,

this astonished fluency of touch;
as if, each time we make love on the hand-woven blanket,

it is again the first time,
and all we have hoarded we burn.

Komorebi

Between the world and the word
are three small shapes,
the signs for 'tree', 'escape' and 'sun'.

I watch how the light leaks through them,
casting a shade in both directions
in the late year, on the russet path

barred with the shadows of trees.
I love how it exults, like any escapee,
on the lake in slow reflective waves,

in radiant bands ascending the birch trunks
according to some unknown frequency,
and in the cormorant extending his wet wings to it

in a messianic gesture,
as if dazzled to absolute
by the word and the world's beauty.

NOTES TO POEMS

The italicised questions at lines 23–25 are taken from the short story 'Canon Alberic's Scrapbook' by M. R. James.

THE MAN WITH NO NAME AS VITAL PRINCIPLE: A GHAZAL

The phrase 'staring their tragic arias' in line 3 refers to Richard Jameson's review of *A Fistful of Dollars* in which he remarks that the movie 'may be described as an opera in which arias are not sung but stared' (*Film Comment*, Vol. 9 [2], Mar–April 1973).

CHIUNE SUGIHARA

Chiune Sugihara (1900–1986) was Vice-Consul to the Empire of Japan in Lithuania during World War II. Against orders, he issued thousands of transit visas to Jewish refugees wishing to escape persecution. In 1985 he was named Righteous Among the Nations by the state of Israel in recognition of his actions.

THE AIRSHIP ERA

This poem, and in particular line 26, are indebted to my reading *of Dr Eckener's Dream Machine: The Historic Saga of the Round-the-World Zeppelin*, by Douglas Botting.

EVERYTHING FLOWERS

The quotation at lines 5–7 is attributed to Arthur C. Clarke in *Visions: How Science Will Revolutionize the 21st Century and Beyond* (1998) by Michio Kaku.

'Komorebi' is a Japanese word which is used to describe the effect of sunlight filtering through the branches and leaves of trees. It has no exact English translation.

ACKNOWLEDGEMENTS

Acknowledgements are due to the editors of the following publications, in which some of these poems first appeared: *The Eagle, Femmes d'Irlande en Poésie* (ed. Clíona Ní Ríordáin), *The Irish Times, Ploughshares, A Poetry Congeries, Poetry, Poetry Ireland Review, Southword,* and *World Literature Today.*

'Spanish Fly', 'Baltic Amber' and 'Blue Poles' were commissioned by Mermaid Arts Centre, Bray, Co. Wicklow, as part of a residency in 2012–2013.

The author gratefully acknowledges a Bursary in Literature received from the Arts Council of Ireland / An Chomhairle Ealaíon for the period 2011–2012, without which this book could not have been completed.

Many thanks to Ally Acker and Neil Hegarty for their invaluable help in reading and responding to earlier manuscript versions of this book.